THIS JOURNAL BELONGS TO

_____

THE
GREEN
JOURNAL

A PERSONAL PLANBOOK OF
ECO-FRIENDLY TIPS AND IDEAS

PHIPPS CONSERVATORY AND BOTANICAL GARDENS

st. lynn's
press

PITTSBURGH

The Green Journal
A Personal Planbook of Eco-Friendly Tips and Ideas

ISBN-13: 978-0-9800288-0-5

Library of Congress Control Number: 2008922390
CIP information available upon request

First Edition, 2008

St. Lynn's Press, POB 18680, Pittsburgh, PA 15236
412.466.0790 . www.stlynnspress.com

Typesetting—Holly Wensel, Network Printing Services
Cover design—Jeff Nicoll
Editor—Abby Dees

Printed in the United States of America
on recycled paper ♲

This title and all of St. Lynn's Press books may be purchased for educational, business, or sales promotional use. For information please write:
Special Markets Department, St. Lynn's Press,
POB 18680, Pittsburgh, PA 15236

10 9 8 7 6 5 4 3 2 1

The Green Journal

It's all over the news: global warming, water shortages, loss of biodiversity, endangered plants and animals, overflowing landfills. It can seem overwhelming. But there are things we can do. Caring for the earth begins by taking action at home.

By making changes in our lifestyle choices, we can improve the environment in our own community and other parts of the world. From how you take care of your lawn and garden, to what you buy, how you travel, and where you volunteer your time, you can make a difference.

The hardest part may simply be changing the way we think about the earth's resources. We've heard all our lives that we live in the land of plenty, but now we're beginning to see that there's a downside to this. Sure, the earth's gifts are wonderfully abundant, but we are using them up faster than they can be replenished. And then what? Nothing we throw away when we're done using it really goes away. It's time for all of us to take a thoughtful look at how we go about our daily lives, remembering that everything we consume uses resources. It's time for each of us to ask ourselves and our families, do we really need it? Is there a better alternative? The good news is that every single choice we make adds up in the end and matters. Most wonderful journeys have modest beginnings. Many great achievements began with the thought, "Maybe if I just tried this instead…"

Ignorance is not bliss; we need to ask questions and then take action. We owe it to the other species on the planet and to the generations that follow us to make sure that they have access to the same resources that we do. So share the earth and use its gifts wisely! The time is now.

This journal contains 12 essays and 6 dozen tips from the spectrum of eco-friendly thought. They are designed to spark this sort of thinking and to gently challenge you to take the next step, whatever it may be. In between, there's space to reflect, make your action plan, or jot down more ideas that you discover. No matter where you are on your own green journey, this journal will, hopefully, become a trusted companion.

Along the way, we will share with you some of the ideas that have informed our choices at Phipps Conservatory and Botanical Gardens and in our own homes. Many of the suggestions are simple things that can be done easily; others will take a greater effort and commitment. In many cases we have included web links to other organizations that will provide more information. You can also check our website (www.phipps.conservatory.org) for new and updated tips. We hope you enjoy your new Journal and that it inspires you to make changes in your lifestyle.

Richard V. Piacentini
Executive Director
Phipps Conservatory and Botanical Gardens

MONTH

CHARGED UP

❦

Chargers for cell phones
and other electronic
devices use energy
even when they're not
being used, so unplug
them when you're
all charged up.

TV Vampires

Plasma TV's might be the worst energy vampires out there. In "standby mode" alone, a plasma display uses about $160 worth of electricity a year. If you've got a Plasma TV, turn it off at the power strip when you're done watching and you'll cut that power drain way down.

SMART MAINTENANCE

Increase the efficiency
of your appliances by
keeping them clean.
Regular maintenance
for your heating and
cooling unit is the
key to keeping it
eco-friendly. Replace
your filters and
clean those
condensers regularly!

THINK SMALL

Everywhere in your house, try to use the smallest appliance you can get away with; for example, to heat small portions, use a toaster oven instead of the big oven. But you probably already do that!

DRYING FOR FREE

Line drying uses free solar energy and eliminates one of your home's biggest energy hogs, the clothes dryer. So why not put your clothes on a diet and get some of that free energy?

THE 411 ON COAL

With all the talk of foreign oil, it's easy to forget that most of our electrical power comes from coal. Burning coal is the dirtiest way to make electricity. To see if your electricity is made from coal from mountain-top removal – the most destructive kind of coal mining – go to www.ilovemountains.org.

Home Energy Conservation

Are you running out of places to plug things in? Does it seem like you have a lot more glowing and beeping gizmos in your life now than you used to? Are cars looking bigger every year? You're not imagining things – our lifestyle really is using more and more energy all the time. But you *can* reduce your energy use without going back to the 20th century. A few simple changes start a great ripple effect: Less carbon dioxide (CO_2) goes into the atmosphere, which slows down global warming and saves you money.

Stay warm. If you were to look at a thermal image of a typical American home you'd see a whole lot of heat leaking through the windows and doors. That might as well be dollar bills flying out. Keep the heat where it belongs – inside – by insulating your ceilings, roof, exterior walls and even floors that are over unheated areas. The cost of installation will come back to you in months, not years. Finish the job right by weather-stripping and caulking your windows and doors. If you're remodeling, go for the double-paned windows with "Low-E" coatings and window frames made from non-conductive materials. Storm windows over your existing windows and radiant heating systems are great options too.

There's no need to heat a room you're not living in. Just close it up and shut the heater vent. And if you've got nice, cozy blankets (or a dog or warm friend), nudge the heater down at night. A programmable thermostat can make all those adjustments automatic. Other easy tricks: Insulate your water heater and turn the temperature down to 120 degrees, install curtains with a radiant heat barrier, and don't use a fireplace to heat your home (save that for romantic evenings).

Cool down. Before you turn on your A/C, give natural ventilation a chance. Open the windows and let the evening breeze in as the sun goes down. Ceiling or whole-house fans are great for cooling a stuffy space. Of course there may be times when you just have to crank up the A/C: Several strategically placed room-sized air conditioners are actually more efficient than a whole-house system. As with heating, a programmable thermostat will tailor your use to your needs. With cooling and heating, it really is a matter of degrees. Try to keep things at a comfortable 78 degrees in the summertime (after all, you can't run around the house naked if you're living in an arctic ice cave). Cool air, like hot air, escapes mostly through doors and windows, so your caulking and insulation will pay off year-round. Finally, check your windows to the south and west – this is a major source of heat buildup during the summer. Easy fix: Put up some nice curtains or plant trees to block the sun.

Be light smart. The best way you can dramatically decrease your energy usage right now is to replace *every light you have* with equivalent compact fluorescents or LED's. They're more expensive than regular lights, but they'll pay for themselves many times over. Remember, these aren't your grandpa's harsh old flickering bulbs. New fluorescent technology is warm and pleasant, and LED's are the cutting-edge lighting designers' light of choice. You can cut your lighting bill by as much as 75%.

Stop the energy vampires. So back to those glowing gizmos: If you turn an electronic item off and you can still see something lit up - a red light or a display panel – it's sucking energy. Most new electronic devices default to "standby mode" (let's call it "vampire mode") and never *really* turn off. Stop that leak by plugging all your gadgets into a power strip that you can switch off manually when you're finished. Some new power strips will even do this for you!

Global warming really does start at your electrical socket. Are you ready to unplug it?

MONTH

Fresh Water Facts

We use fresh water faster than the earth can replenish and clean it, so by saving water we ensure that there's enough fresh water for plants and animals and we save energy by reducing the use of water treatment facilities. Water conservation helps prevent pollution and keeps the earth healthy and clean.

KEEP IT HOT

❧

Insulate water pipes to reduce the amount of water that is wasted while waiting for it to heat at the tap. And wrap your water heater with an insulating blanket; or better yet, install a tankless water heater right at the sink and the water will be hot instantly.

TOILET LEAKS

Check to see if your toilet leaks by putting 10 drops of food coloring in the tank. Wait 45 minutes, and check the water in the bowl. If you see color, the toilet is leaking.

GARDEN TIP

Save water in your
garden by mulching
around the bases of your
plants. This will help
keep their roots moist for
a longer period of time
than plants surrounded
by bare soil or lawn.

DRIP, DRIP...

❦

Many leaks in your house
are not very noticeable,
so here's a good way to
know if you're losing
water to leaks: Write
down the numbers on
your water meter, wait
two hours without using
any water and then look
at the numbers again. If
the two numbers don't
match exactly, you
have a leak. According
to the Environmental
Protection Agency,
dripping faucets and
other minor leaks can
waste over 2,000 gallons
of water each year!

ROLL OUT
THE BARRELS

Redirect water from
your gutters into a
rain barrel or two.
You'll be surprised how
quickly they will fill
on a rainy day. Use this
to water your garden.
Put moisture-loving
varieties near the
rain barrels to make
watering easy.

Water Conservation

Every water-saving choice we make has the potential to save thousands of gallons of water each year. Here's how you can make your home water friendly:

Did you know that the most effective single water-saving choice you can make is to install inexpensive aerators to your faucets? Available at hardware stores, aerators cut usage from 3 to 4 gallons per minute to as little as 1/2 a gallon, without sacrificing pressure. You won't be able to tell the difference, but you'll be using up to 88% less water. In the bathroom sink, choose an aerator that produces 1 gallon per minute, but for the kitchen, go for a flow rate of 2 gallons per minute.

In the bathroom: A cheap and easy way to make your older toilet more efficient is to put bricks or plastic bottles (filled with water and a few rocks or a handful of sand) in the tank, away from the flushing mechanism. Just remember to leave at least 3 gallons of water in older tanks for the toilet to work properly. This little trick will save more than 10 gallons of water a day. Better yet, replace your toilet with a newer model that uses just 1.6 gallons per flush. And if you're ready to go the extra mile, purchase a composting toilet. No, it won't stink up your bathroom, but it *will* reduce the amount of water that you use per flush to just 1/5 to 1/3 of a gallon. That is a savings of up to 95%, and a great conversation piece too!

Low-flow shower heads have been improved lately, resulting in higher efficiency with no reduction in water pressure. They'll save an average of 8,000 gallons of water each year. And how about challenging your family to limiting showers to 5 minutes?

In the kitchen: Fill up those machines! Only run the dishwasher with a full load. Same for the washing machine, and if you use cold water for lightly soiled loads, you'll save energy too.

If you're running lots of water down the drain while waiting for it to cool down or warm up, place a bowl or bucket in the sink to catch it and use it for other things, like making coffee, soaking dirty pots or watering houseplants. Similarly, limit your use of the garbage disposal. How about starting a compost pile for kitchen waste instead? – you'll get wonderful soil for your garden. If you wash dishes by hand, don't let the water run. Instead, partially fill the sink with warm, soapy water, and rinse dishes under a faucet fitted with an aerator – two little changes with big results. Another great change is to install a water filter instead of using bottled water, which is surprisingly wasteful and also uses lots of energy as it's shipped from place to place (think Fiji or New Zealand), and then to your door.

In the yard: How many times have you seen sprinklers turned on in the full heat of the day? Or doing a thorough job watering the sidewalk? Millions of gallons of water are wasted each year by incorrect sprinkler use. Drip irrigation will make sure that water goes right to the roots, where it's need. Watering between dawn and 9:00 AM will ensure that water doesn't evaporate and that you won't invite pests and disease from watering at night. And remember, windy days and watering just don't go together well.

For the hardcore conserver, consider capturing the grey water in your home (water from sinks and showers) to use for irrigation. Check to see if your hometown allows this. And for you swimmers, cover the pool when not in use to limit water loss from evaporation.

Which water choices are you ready to make today? Each one will make a world of difference for you, your family, and your planet.

MONTH

LAWNS ARE LOVELY, BUT…

So are lots of other types of groundcover – many of which are quite low maintenance too, and use far less water. Try mixing and matching in your garden, and only planting lawn where you really need it.

How Much Water?

If you occasionally
water your lawn with
a sprinkler, place
containers (pans or
mugs, etc.) evenly over
the area, and time how
long it takes for them
to fill to 1 inch. That's
all you need for a good,
thorough watering; any
less will encourage a
shallow root system that
can't resist drought, and
any more is wasteful.

Soil Rx

❧

Do a soil test every three years to learn about the nutrients and chemical composition of your soil. Soil test kits are available through your local land grant university. Once you have an accurate "portrait" of your soil you can make the best choices to correct deficiencies and help your garden thrive.

Fresh Start?

If your lawn is full of weeds, it may be time for a new and improved version. Remove all grass and weeds, add organic amendments to the soil, and reseed.

GIVE YOUR
MOWER A REST

🌿

Try the No Mow lawn
mix if it will work in
your climate. It grows
very slowly and looks
natural and informal.

HELLO, GOOD BUGS!

Once you swear off
the chemicals, it may
take a few years for
earthworms and other
helpful creatures to come
back, but hang in there
– it will be worth the
wait! There are dozens
(hundreds?) of beneficial
bugs that will be your
garden allies for years
to come, and make
you glad you retired
those chemicals.

Organic Lawn Care

Can you be green and still have a beautiful lawn? It's easier than you may think:

For new lawns, use one of the new turf-type tall fescues or perennial rye grasses, many of which are resistant to drought, insects and disease. Some turf grasses are "endophyte-enhanced;" in other words, they're infected with friendly fungi that work symbiotically with the grass to make it more resistant to insects and able to compete well with weeds.

Groom your lawn. Get a jump on weeds by planting in early fall. Once your lawn is established, regular mowing is your best tool for keeping it healthy. Always use a sharp blade! Mow to about 3" for most grasses; this helps the roots grow deeper, making your lawn more resistant to drought. In shady areas, mow an inch higher to create more surface area for photosynthesis. Try not to cut off more than 1/3 of the grass blade. This way you can leave the clippings in place – they'll start decomposing right away and add valuable nitrogen to the soil. Good mowing will give you a thick, weed-resistant lawn.

Give it a drink. Ideally, natural rainfall should provide all the water you need. It's normal for most grasses to go dormant during summer – they'll come back when the rain does. During prolonged droughts, though, it's a good idea to give your lawn infrequent, deep watering.

Compost! Fertilize once in the spring and once in the fall, using organic fertilizer. To minimize crabgrass and other annual weeds, use corn gluten in spring. Each fall, cover your lawn with a thin layer (less than 3/8") of compost or topsoil. This will add beneficial microorganisms and bury fungal spores, preventing disease. If any thatch has accumulated, this will also help to break it down.

Keep it tidy. If thatch is less than 1/2", it's fine, but thicker thatch means something is wrong. The main culprits are over-fertilization or the use of chemicals that inadvertently harm the good bacteria, fungi and earthworms that continuously break thatch down. Special equipment is available to remove thatch – something else you can do in the fall.

While you're at it, check to see if your soil has become too compacted; compaction decreases beneficial microbial activity and keeps roots sparse and shallow. You may need to aerate to keep your lawn healthy and resistant to weed invasion. Use an aerator that removes plugs of soil, which can then be broken up and left on the lawn where they will naturally break down.

Always over-seed any bare spots whenever they appear, before weeds have a chance to come in.

Mix it up. Consider whether those weeds are really so bad. Some "weeds," such as violets, add lovely color and texture. White clover used to be an integral part of grass seed mixes because it adds nitrogen to the soil.

Organic methods should eliminate diseases and insects. These tips will make your lawn robust and allow lawn-friendly bugs to thrive. But if a problem comes up, resist the urge to reach for toxic chemicals!

So how about spending a day with your lawn, making it happy, healthy and truly green?

MONTH

ON THE MOVE

Don't throw stuff away
just because you're
on the move. Keep a
spare bag in your car
for recycling all those
cans, bottles, and
windshield fliers that
wind up in your back
seat. On vacation? Toss
a recycling bag into your
suitcase and keep your
hotel room green.

PAPER OR PLASTIC? HOW ABOUT NEITHER...

❧

Plastic bags are made from petroleum and can take 1000 years to break down. And even though paper bags are compostable, they use a lot of resources to make. Take your own cloth or canvas bags to the market next time – some stores even offer a discount if you bring your own.

USE YOUR VOICE

Over 30% of landfill space is taken up with packaging materials. Be an advocate for the earth and go right to the source: Let the manufacturers of your favorite products know that you want recycled and less wasteful packaging from now on.

JUNK THE JUNK MAIL

❧

Wouldn't it be nice to get less junk mail and save a few trees? Call 1-888-5OPT OUT to reduce all those annoying credit card offers. Any time you donate money, fill out a warranty card or order something through the mail, write "please do not sell my name or address" in big letters. Most folks will oblige.

THOSE OLD
PAINT CANS
🍂

Dispose of paint by
using it up. If just a
small amount remains,
give your wall another
quick coat. If you have
a lot of paint, call
your local high school
and ask if their theater
department could
use it for painting
props and sets.

PARTY FAVORS

Parties don't have to leave you up to your ears in landfill. Put out special recycling bins for cans, bottles and paper. For gifts, use leftover wrapping paper, paper bags or even the comics section of the newspaper. This type of re-gifting saves trees, and your friends will think you're a green Martha Stewart.

Reduce/Reuse/Recycle

Can you imagine a world without plastic? Our great grandparents probably could, because plastic, as we know it, is not even a hundred years old. Plastic brought with it a whole new idea: disposable things. Now, a century later, we've learned that nothing's really disposable. But there are ways to manage our stuff that will keep the earth from becoming a big round landfill:

Reduce. Ideally, the mantra of any aspiring greenie should be "buy only what I need," whether it's a dress, a book or a car. But it's hard to be perfect in our consumer-driven culture. Even if you were "born to shop," pause before you swipe your credit card and think about the energy and resources that went into making and bringing that item to you. If you decide you'd rather bank the money, or buy a "green certificate" (see "Voting with Your Dollars"), you'll feel great and tame the shopoholic beast. The flip side of this is to buy in bulk to reduce wasteful packaging – just make sure you use what you buy!

Reuse. When it is time to buy, look for items that can be reused. Think of "disposable" as another word for low quality. Andy Warhol turned soup cans into art, so how about turning an old boot into a planter? They really don't make 'em like they used to so instead of tossing out old things, find out if they can be repaired. Soon they won't be old, but "retro." And remember: Your trash may be someone else's treasure. Nearly all your furniture, clothes, appliances or car (even surplus or used building materials!) can be donated to someone. Just call and ask.

Recycle. When it's time to say goodbye, then it's time to recycle and ease the burden on our landfills. Currently, 50% of paper, 34% of plastic soft drink bottles, 45% of aluminum, and 67% of major appliances are recycled in the US. This is wonderful progress, but we've still got a long way to go. If you have roadside collection, follow the rules for your community faithfully! This will keep the errant greasy pizza box from contaminating an otherwise great cache of recycling. For items that your trash company doesn't pick up, go to www.earth911.org to see where you can take them.

So many things can be recycled: Aluminum products (cans, siding, furniture, etc.) and glass have an almost infinite number of lives in recycled form. Because it requires so much energy to produce aluminum from ore, it's a wonderful material to recycle. And recycled glass items take 40% less energy to produce than new ones do.

Over 3 billion batteries are sold each year in the US (and counting). Batteries contain heavy metals, including mercury, metal hydride and lead acid, which leach from landfills and vaporize into the air. This is a toxic problem, so when you can, use rechargeable batteries and recycle the rest. Never throw a battery away.

Over 180 million gallons of motor oil are illegally dumped each year, on the ground, down a storm drain or in the trash, where it seeps into the soil, sea and groundwater. Alarming fact: One gallon of used oil can contaminate 1 million gallons of water. Drain old oil into its original container or a jug (just make sure it never held cleaners, solvents or bleach) and take it, along with used oil filters, to an oil-change center that recycles. With the price of oil at record highs, recycling the oil we've got makes good sense – most of it goes toward countless manufacturing and industrial applications. If you're feeling *really* motivated, you can even buy recycled car oil for your car (at a premium, alas).

It comes right down to thinking about all our stuff a little differently. It's supposed to benefit us, not weigh us – or the earth – down. So, what would you like to do next to lighten your load?

MONTH

68/78

In the office, keep
temperatures at a
comfortable 68 in
the winter and 78 in
the summer. If that
is what everyone
expects, they will
dress accordingly.

COMPUTER TIMEOUT

When you will be away
from your desk for a
while, or when you're off
at lunch, turn off your
computer and monitor.
Shutting down only your
monitor is good, but
shutting down the whole
thing is even better. And
whenever possible, use
power-saving modes on
your computer.

LOCAL IS GOOD

❧

Encourage your café
or cafeteria to carry
local and organic foods.
You'll be eating better
and healthier, and
you'll be saving all that
energy/fuel that trucks
in those faraway foods.

PAPER SAVER

Print on both sides
of paper whenever
possible. Many
printers will do
this automatically.

SICK BUILDING SYNDROME?

Modern buildings are often designed to be airtight, with windows that don't open for natural ventilation; this leads to unhealthy buildups of interior toxins. Fight the syndrome by filling your office with plants! Ficus, spider plants and Boston fern, along with many others, cleanse the air of common toxins. See www.coopext.colostate. edu/4DMG/Plants/clean. html for a list of plants that can keep your workplace clean.

ALTERNATIVE COMMUTING

❧

Encourage employees
to bike or bus to work
by offering a small
salary credit, showers
and bike racks. You'll
not only help the
environment, you'll help
your employees stay
healthy and fit. Consider
providing premium
parking spots for those
who carpool or drive
efficient cars.

At Work

You can be green at work whether you're an employee or the boss. If you're the boss, your green choices set an example for your entire staff, who will not only respect your commitment to the earth, they'll take their eco-knowledge home (that's the green multiplier effect). As an employee, you can encourage your company to go green and make money along the way. Here's how you can make your business pay off for the planet:

Build green. If you're building or leasing a new facility, check out the US Green Building Council (www.usgbc.org) for info on LEED-certified buildings. LEED (Leadership in Energy and Environmental Design) certification is *the* standard for energy efficiency and can save money through lower energy bills, fewer work-related illnesses, and greater staff retention.

Just like at home. Encourage people to turn lights off when an office is not being used. Put up signs next to the light switches – and don't forget the restroom! Switch to filtered water, rather than bottled, to save energy and all those plastic bottles. For maximum savings, put aerators on your faucets and consider installing a waterless, flush-less urinal. These fancy gizmos save up to 45,000 gallons of water a year and are hygienic and odor-free.

Some energy choices will take small up-front investments, but the company's bottom line will quickly get back in the black and earning a nice return. Swapping incandescent bulbs for compact fluorescents can save up to 75% in lighting costs, and Energy Star computer monitors use between 25–60% less electricity than standard models. At night, shut computers down all the way instead of putting them into "sleep" mode.

Green your power. For the rest of your energy needs, ask your utility company about purchasing electricity from renewable sources. You can also buy carbon offsets or "green certificates" (see "Voting with Your Dollars"). This is a great way to help compensate for the CO_2 produced by corporate travel. Yes, it's an expense, but think of it as innovative advertising: A well-publicized investment in renewable energy will establish your business as responsible and forward thinking. Check out www.greentagsusa.org or www.nativeenergy.com.

Pay attention to paper. Our "paperless" offices are going through more trees than ever. Keep trees growing by going digital for your presentations and using your email for handling documents. Send out meeting notes ahead of time by email and then project them overhead for discussion. And instead of using hard-copy faxes, use a web-based fax service or send documents in PDF format. For hard copies, use only 100% recycled, non-chlorine paper – it looks great nowadays.

Make recycling easy. Just about everything in an office can be recycled: paper, cardboard, printer and toner cartridges, glass and plastic bottles and soda cans. The surest way to get people to recycle is to give them easily accessible bins. Along with a few, gentle reminders, people will soon get into the habit. And keep the break room from becoming an ecological black hole by eliminating Styrofoam cups, plastic plates and utensils and anything else that's disposable – it's even better than recycling.

On a personal note. See if you can break up with your dry cleaner. This will spare the environment a lot of toxic chemical waste, and so will buying organic cotton, which high-end designers are using more and more.

As you make these changes, let people know what you're up to and why. You might just become on office hero! Are you ready to wave the green banner proudly from your office door?

MONTH

GROW GRANNY-STYLE

Get to know about
heirloom varieties of
flowers and vegetables.
And check out the
"open-pollinated"
varieties (meaning
they're not patented
hybrids). They have
interesting histories,
and their seeds can be
saved and replanted
year after year.

HOMEGROWN GOODIES

Grow your own
vegetables and
herbs. You can even
incorporate edible
plants in among your
ornamental flower beds.
And if the only space
you have is a patio or a
porch, plant your veggies
in pots. You'll be amazed
at how prolific a potted
tomato plant can be!
You actually save energy
by growing your own
food because dinner only
travels from as far as
your back yard.

Invite Some Friends

Be a friend to bees and bugs; there are so many beneficial insects. We are in the middle of a major bee-loss epidemic worldwide, and without these pollinators many flowering plants would suffer! Provide pollinator habitat by planting flowers with your vegetables and letting some weeds thrive on the edge of your garden.

ORGANIC FERTILIZERS

Synthetic fertilizers are often made from petroleum and may also contain chemical insecticides and weed killers. Best to use only organic fertilizers, thereby contributing to the long-term health of your garden – and your children and pets.

SMART WATER USE

If you're starting a new garden or replacing older plants, consider using drought-resistant varieties. They're fabulous water misers. Your local nursery can advise. You'll also save water by adding lots of organic matter to the soil.

KEEP IT CASUAL

You can reduce the
use of powered garden
equipment by letting
shrubs and hedges grow
naturally, rather than by
pruning them into formal
designs. The good news
is that many of the old
favorites are available
in dwarf varieties,
eliminating the problem
of "shrubs gone wild."

Sustainable Gardening

With just a little bit of smart choosing, you can have a garden that is both beautiful and good for the environment. The basics are simple:

The right plant in the right place. This is the sustainable gardener's motto. First, find plants that will grow in your region without the need for additional water, pesticides or synthetic fertilizers. They can be native or exotic (meaning they're not from these parts). A word of caution about exotics: Check first with your state department of natural resources to make sure that you're not about to introduce an invasive species that will overpower and displace native plants. An extreme example is the kudzu, a pretty Japanese vine that came here innocently enough, but now costs the U.S. a half billion dollars each year to control.

Next, take a good look at your garden site and study its conditions. Is it sunny or shady, wet or dry? Does it get gentle morning sunlight or intense afternoon rays? When you've figured out your garden's characteristics, select a plant that will grow the best with the least amount of assistance. There are lots of good online sources of information.

Be water conscious. You can save water by growing drought-tolerant species; just be sure to give them a good, healthy start by irrigating regularly for the first few weeks. If need be later on, water by hand or with a well-placed drip system.

Go old school. Once your garden is in the ground and growing, take care of it the old-fashioned way: Avoid using gas-powered equipment. These tools waste fossil fuels and put CO_2 and other pollutants into the air. It may seem ridiculously retro, but why not use a rake and a push-mower instead? It's a great workout. But if you really need those machines, look into electric alternatives. Remember, of course, that the best electricity is made from renewable resources.

Avoid those chemicals! Integrated Pest Management, or IPM, is a great way to get rid of bugs and weeds without hurting the earth or your plants. In IPM, you identify the problem and zero in on it, rather than treating your whole garden and lawn – and you always use the least toxic approach first. For example, a burst of water from the hose will often get rid of offending insects, or you can cut the infected area out. The next step might be beneficial insects or a safer pesticide, like horticultural oil. Pesticide alternatives can be found at the aptly named www.beyondpesticides.org.

Compost is key. Apply lots of organic matter – a nice way of saying "use compost and manure." Organic matter provides rich nutrients for your garden. If you work it into the soil when you're planting, your seedlings will grow up to be strong and healthy plants. Two to three inches of organic matter applied as mulch will help suppress weed growth and conserve soil moisture by cutting down on evaporation. You can also make your own compost (and feel very virtuous). Really, you can compost almost anything that grows from the earth: leaves and other garden waste, wilted flower arrangements, or organic fruits and veggies you never got around to eating. Composting is easy and turns waste into wonderful living things. You'll spare the landfills and save money in organic mulch; it's also a way to get the whole family involved in a healthy project with a tangible payoff.

Organic gardening is a great way of saying that you care about the earth and its gifts. Are you ready to grow your garden green?

MONTH

GET CRAFTY

Green is fun when it becomes a messy crafts project. Let kids create elaborate "Turn It Off" signs that they can put up by light switches, computers and electronics.

RECYCLING TOGETHER

Encourage kids to save lightly used paper in a handy scrap box at the front of the class. They can use it later for art projects and jotting down their green ideas (it's also good for those kids who chronically forget their notebooks).

When it's time to throw papers away, put recycling bins where kids can easily use them. This helps them develop good green habits.

MAKE THE SWITCH

Encourage school administrators to switch to Energy Star rated computer monitors and to swap out energy-sucking incandescent light bulbs for efficient fluorescents.

COMPOSTING IDEA

Collect organic lunch remains like banana peels and apple cores from the lunchroom and cafeteria, and then deposit them in a school compost bin. Kids will love watching their teachers dig their hands into a "gross" pile of slimy gunk weeks later, only to learn that it's become nutrient-dense, fresh fertilizer.

GO, GREEN GARDENERS, GO!

Ask your school to donate a dedicated space on campus grounds for a student garden club. (That's where the compost from the cafeteria will end up.) With faculty supervision, the kids will do everything required to make their garden thrive, from deciding between fruits, veggies or native plants to throwing an organic bake sale to raise money for seeds and supplies.

Kids and Schools

Wouldn't it be wonderful if, right alongside math, history and literature, we taught our kids about protecting their planet? Teachers and parents can get the ball rolling by sharing their green ideas with teachers, administrators and school board officials:

Encourage nature literacy. Our brains need oxygen to function, so give kids some fresh air! An outdoor classroom brings a whole new perspective to a subject, whether as an alternative space for discussing poetry or for hands-on lessons in science and math. If adults step up, nature really can compete with video games and MySpace.

Get them composting. Composting puts the 3R's (reduce, reuse and recycle) into practice and teaches the cycle of life. A classroom compost bin gives children the opportunity to watch nature's recycling team of bacteria and worms (every kid secretly loves worms) turn food waste, leaves and other organic materials into "black gold" for the school garden. The gardeners at Cornell University (www.css. cornell.edu/compost/schools.html) offer tips for integrating a compost bin into classroom exercises.

Bring the farm to school. It's hard to fight childhood obesity and diabetes when the cafeteria serves french fries and sugary drinks. Proper nutrition is integrally linked to healthy brain function, which is why, since 2000, schools around the country have adopted Farm to School programs (www.farmtoschool.org). Farm to School encourages healthy, sustainable eating habits in school cafeterias and teaches schools how to put locally grown, whole foods on the menu.

Bring the school to the farm. Kids love field trips, so how about taking students to the farm to meet the folks who produce their food? When they get back to school, they'll be pumped up and motivated to plan and plant their own organic garden as a class project. To a kid (or anyone else) a carrot tastes like heaven when you've grown it yourself.

Get on the green bus. If your district uses diesel-powered busses, ask the school board to require drivers to turn off their engines while waiting for students to board. You can also talk to them about using cleaner fuels. (The EPA offers more information: www.epa.gov/ebt-pages/pollenergycleanfuels.html). And while you're talking about pollution control, educate your school about safe cleaning products. One out of every three cleaning chemicals in US schools is known to cause human health or environmental problems. Check out www.greenseal.org to find alternative products that are approved for the people and the earth.

Meet the Green Squad! Kids learn best when they can discover problems and solutions on their own, so ask kids to study their schools' environmental behavior and then help them brainstorm eco-friendly alternatives. The National Resources Defense Council (www.nrdc.org/greensquad/) offers fact sheets that help teachers and students identify environmental problems at school.

Make every subject green. The green curriculum is multidisciplinary, touching on everything from geography, biology, math and cultural studies. You can use green concepts to teach almost anything. For example, calculate how many miles a local apple travels compared to one from Chile. The Center for Ecoliteracy (www.ecoliteracy.org) has lots more green lesson ideas.

Do as I say, and as I do! For better or worse, children learn as much from watching adults as they do from the chalkboard. Teach green through example, and then talk to your children about your choices. Our children may be the best earth advocates we have, so what green wisdom would you like to pass on to them today?

MONTH

THE GOODS ON YOUR GOODS

🌿

Find out how clean or how toxic your cosmetics and personal care products are at www.ewg.org. If it's toxic for you, it's probably toxic for the environment.

FISH ON FRIDAY?

Are you concerned about making the most environmentally friendly fish choices? The Monterey Bay Aquarium has the information you need. Just visit www.mbayaq.org. Wondering about mercury levels in your fish? Check out www.nrdc.org or www.gotmercury.org.

A Rose by Any Other Name...

Did you know the majority of cut flowers sold in the US are imported from growers in developing countries where they may use pesticides that are banned in other countries? They can be bad for the workers who handle them and bad for you. But you don't have to give up beautiful cut flowers in order to be green; just choose organic. Check the origins and ask questions.

PLASTIC BY THE NUMBERS

❦

That little triangle stamped into plastic goods can tell you a lot: When you buy plastic, #1 or #2 is best for recycling. Some areas will recycle #4 and #5 too. Avoid #3, #6 and #7 – they're considered unsafe. PVC and vinyl are #3, and it's the most toxic plastic on the market today!

FRESHENING UP

If want to give your home a nice, fresh coat of paint, use paint with low levels of volatile organic compounds (VOC's). Or if you're about to buy that wild new shag rug, choose a carpet made from recycled materials.

FUN WITH FLOORING

Bamboo, cork and
linoleum flooring are a
little more expensive
then vinyl flooring, but
they're less toxic, from
renewable resources,
and very stylish.

Voting with your Dollars

Along with voting for representatives who share your concern for the earth, you can also get your point across by using your wallet. How you spend your money speaks loudly and clearly about what's important to you. Here are a few ways to use the marketplace to help the environment:

Purchase green power. The generation of electricity accounts for about 40% of the CO_2 released into the atmosphere and only 2% of our electricity comes from renewable resources. But in some areas local utility companies offer electricity produced from renewable resources, such as wind and solar power – find out if yours does too. Even if they haven't "seen the light," you can still invest in green energy through Renewable Energy Certificates (or "Green Certificates"). These tradable commodities encourage clean power by subsidizing the sustainable generation of electricity. Visit www.eere.energy.gov/greenpower or www.green-e.org.

Buy fair trade. When you buy a fairly traded good you demonstrate that the responsible production of food and other items matters to you. These products include everything from coffee and tea to chocolate and even fresh flowers. Next time you're at your local market, look for fair trade labels, or check out TransFair USA at www.transfairusa.org to see what other responsibly produced goods are available.

Make wise food choices. Your grocery list makes a statement about our soil, water and energy resources, so change over to locally produced foods and labels that say "organic" (or for coffee, tea and chocolate, "shade grown"). Not only is it better for you – and tastier – it's better for the environment. To get the "organic" label, food must meet strict government requirements. Look carefully, though, because terms like "natural" or "free-range" are not regulated.

Eating less meat saves energy and water: If you do eat meat, visit www.certifiedhumane.com for farms that raise animals humanely. The big factory farms generally don't, and this results in excessive use of antibiotics, which can lead to antibiotic resistance. Factory farming also creates about 500,000 tons of environmental pollution a year in the US.

OK, you get the picture! The less energy, water and chemicals that go into transporting and processing your food, the better. Sometimes it's not the cheapest way to go, but your grocery money will feed your family and help build a greener economy. That's like a double-coupon for the environment.

Look for the logo. The Forest Stewardship Council (www.fscus.org) certifies corporations and land managers who agree to grow and harvest their forest products sustainably. When you use FSC-certified wood or paper you are voting for a more sustainable way of using our forest resources and showing your support for environmentally responsible retailers.

Read the label and ask questions about your goods and services – and then support the suppliers that support your views. They'll love you for it.

Bigger isn't always better. Looking for your dream-home? An energy efficient McMansion can waste more resources then a traditional smaller home. But no matter how big your home, you might qualify for federal, state and local incentives if you convert to solar. And any extra energy you make goes right back into the grid, to benefit everyone.

When you spend with the good of the earth in mind you get paid back forever, in clean air, soil and water. What would you like to say with your dollars today?

MONTH

THE WHEEL DEAL

Properly aligned and
inflated tires can save up
to 18 gallons of gas per
year – that's like a free
tank just for being
a responsible car owner.

TOPPING OFF

Did you know that topping off your tank is bad for the environment? When the gas pump shuts off, stop fueling; you'll reduce spills and toxic fumes. Take the next step and avoid refueling at all on Ozone Action Days — more and more towns are implementing "OAD's," so find out if yours is too.

UNDER THE HOOD

❦

A smooth-running
engine will increase
your fuel economy. If
you notice a sudden
drop in your fuel
efficiency, it may
mean that something's
wrong under the hood.
Take care of your car
and you'll take care
of the planet!

FLY/DRIVE?

❧

Going on a long trip?
If it is a 4-hour drive
or less, it's more fuel
efficient to drive than
fly – and no security
officers will be pawing
through your stuff.

Fun on 2 Wheels

Electric bikes and scooters offer the speed of a car (up to 40 miles per hour) and the fuel efficiency of a bike (plug it into a solar charger!). Styles range from old-fashioned cruisers with bells and baskets, to futuristic racers; either way, your commute will be a lot more fun.

WIND POWER

If you vacation on the water, what about trading in your powerboat for a sailboat and discovering just how fast the wind can carry you along the water? What's old is new again, and the kids will love it.

Transportation

In the US, the average automobile creates more than 5½ tons of CO_2 every year. With over 220 million cars and light trucks registered – well, that's a lot of greenhouse gas. So, where to begin? As with most green changes, it's best to start simple. The littlest things will add up fast; soon you'll be reducing your carbon footprint and saving lots of gas money.

Cut down your miles. We all know that taking mass transit, or even better, biking and walking, are the greenest ways to commute, but it's not always practical to dump the car completely. So, ask if folks at work would like to carpool – and get another half hour of sleep in the back seat. If you can, consider moving closer to work; sometimes what you save in fuel expense and time on the road can offset the cost of living closer to town.

If moving isn't an option, you can still drive less and get all your tasks done by combining your goals: Do all your shopping and banking in one trip. After you come home, make sure you empty your car out right away because extra weight decreases gas mileage. And doesn't it sometimes feel like we're in such a rush, we've forgotten how to use our feet? Get back in touch with them by turning local errands into fitness opportunities. When the weather's good, walk your kids to school and get caught up with one another along the way.

You *can* drive 55. Easy changes to your driving style will dramatically increase your gas mileage. Start by turning your car off if it's going to idle for more than a minute. Once you're back on the road try to obey the speed limit. It's sad news for all those green speed demons out there, but you can improve your mileage by 15% if you go 55 MPH instead of 65.

Remember the old story about the tortoise and the hare? It's true for fuel efficiency too: Jackrabbit stops and starts will not get you there any faster, but they will drain your tank in a hurry. As soon as you get to cruising speed, make sure your car is in overdrive (newer models do this automatically). You'll zip along just fine, saving the lower gears for hills and other torque-demanding trips.

Buy a green machine. When it's time for a new car, resist the understandable temptation to order the biggest engine they make. Is 0-60 in 6 seconds really that much better than 7 seconds when you don't live on a racetrack? Check out hybrids too, which are getting more common (and more powerful) with each model year. But hybrids aren't the only game in town: Some gas-only models leave some hybrids in the dust when it comes to low environmental impact. The EPA's online Green Vehicle Guide (www.epa.gov/green-vehicles) provides environmental information on nearly all car models available today.

Once you've chosen your dream car, remember that all those options can add weight, which will cut your gas efficiency by up to a few miles per gallon. The biggest gas-hog options are automatic trans-missions and all-wheel drive – they'll slow you down too.

Share your ride. Car sharing is the hot new alternative to buying the whole enchilada, and it's being done by bazillions of people in Europe and North America. "Zipcar" vehicles are fuel efficient and affordable, and especially good for folks who only need a car occa-sionally (or a bigger car every so often for those special trips). Stud-ies show that each shared car put in service can take up to 15 private cars off the road. This means less pollution, less traffic congestion and competition for parking spaces. Businesses can even open a car-sharing account rather purchasing a whole new fleet of vehicles. Visit www.zipcar.com for information.

How green can you make your next ride?

MONTH

BUTTERFLY GARDENS

Find out which butterflies are native to your area and offer host plants for their larvae and nectar plants for the adults. Pretty soon they'll be making regular stops in your garden.

WINTER SHELTER

Start a brush pile in an out-of-the-way corner of your yard to provide wintering and nesting spaces for a variety of species.

THAT OLD LOG

In a wooded area, allow
at least part of a dead
tree to remain. It will
provide a source of
insects for birds, as
well as cozy space for
cavity nesters.

SKULL AND CROSSBONES

Minimize your use of
pesticides – it can't
be said enough. These
chemicals really do harm
your health and habitat.

Habitat Gardening

As we putter around the house or speed off to work, or even just lie outside in a hammock, it's easy to forget that we are part of a teeming natural habitat – one that is increasingly threatened by pollution, development and plain old bad habits. You can turn things around by turning your garden into a pesticide-free area where flora and fauna can thrive. Most people have no problem attracting deer, rabbits and raccoons (all important parts of our ecosystem), but how about creating a lush haven for lower-profile creatures like toads and salamanders, birds and bees, dragonflies and butterflies? They'll bring vibrant color and life to your home.

The three main components of any habitat are water, shelter and food. If you already have these elements in your yard, you probably see a daily parade of fauna already. If not, it's very easy and inexpensive to build your backyard habitat. Many of these techniques can even work on a porch or balcony. Almost any place can become a thriving habitat.

First, provide a water feature. A birdbath is a great choice – just clean the water every few days to avoid breeding mosquitoes. Or you can go all out and install a pond. A little more effort will attract a lot more wildlife, such as frogs. There's really nothing like the gentle thrum of a dozen contented, ribbiting frogs lounging in a pond, and you can build one in an afternoon. There are some good, simple how-to books available, or just do an Internet search for "build your own pond." Fish and underwater plants will help keep the pond ecosystem balanced and clean; ask your local pond or pet store about the best kind for you.

Next, provide shelter. Animals need places to hide to feel safe and raise their young. If you have shrubs or small trees in your yard, you already have suitable cover. If not, plant some. Small piles of brush, dead branches and leaves create habitat and wintering spots for many animals, birds, and even some butterflies. Other options include making or buying nesting boxes for birds or even building a toad house. Toads don't spend as much time in the water as the average frog, so they'll appreciate a custom home outside the pond. To create a semi-aquatic toad abode, fill a saucer with water and place a clay pot upside down on top, with one edge resting on a rock (this creates a small entryway).

Last, provide food. It's a top critter attraction. Bird feeders lure not only birds, but squirrels and chipmunks as well. Shrubs or trees – especially natives – are both lovely and nutritional. And plants with berries and seeds are very appealing to our feathered friends. Birds will feast on the fruits of these plants, especially during the late fall and winter months, when the ground is too hard for them to pluck out tasty larvae. If you plant flowering annuals and perennials, such as coneflower and zinnias, let them go to seed – soon you'll likely be visited by goldfinches. Many nectar-bearing flowers, from spring through fall, will attract butterflies, hummingbirds and bees.

It should come as no surprise that pesticides and natural habitats aren't very compatible. Birds enjoy grubs, slugs, insects and worms, so if you apply chemicals aimed at killing these things, don't expect a lot of avian house guests.

You're just a few steps away from turning your garden or porch into a beautiful and bustling place. Are you ready to invite some new friends to share your home?

MONTH

All to the Good

❦

Local food is health food. Freshly picked food has much higher nutritional content than well traveled food that has spent time in storage and shipping.

FARMS IN TRANSITION

Even if it's not labeled "organic," the food at your local farmer's market may contain fewer pesticides and chemicals than the produce at your grocery store. Ask the farmer! It's possible that the farm is in transition or hasn't gone through the formal process of being certified organic.

BEST IN SEASON

Remember how good
peaches and berries
tasted when you were
a kid? If you don't,
ask your parents and
grandparents about this
delicious memory. Stores
back then only carried
fruits and veggies when
they were in season
— and at their very
best. Focus on eating
seasonally, and you'll
look forward to all the
treats that come around
just once a year.

ADVENTURES WITH YOUR CSA

When you join a CSA, you'll receive seasonal produce on a regular basis, including fruits and veggies you may never have seen before. Look up recipes for these unusual foods on the Internet and see how far you can expand your palate.

DOWN ON THE FARM

Many local growers
offer pick-your-own days.
It's a great way to teach
your family about where
our food comes from,
and nothing is tastier
than a fresh-picked
strawberry or apple.

FOOD TO BE PROUD OF

Be a local patriot! Purchasing locally grown foods increases food security and keeps additional money in your own community. This creates a more prosperous hometown and reduces risk of food contamination. Each dollar spent locally generates two more dollars in community reinvestment.

Buy Local!

Whether your dinner guests are vegans or omnivores, organic or oblivious, you can find something for everyone if you try to buy local whenever you can. In fact, "buy local" – meaning that your food should be produced within 100 miles of your home – has become the rallying cry of green foodies, and for good reason.

To our inner gourmet, the issue is taste. Most fruit and vegetables are chosen for their hardiness, and flavor is the first thing to go, especially after a 2-week trip to the supermarket. In contrast, local foods are often sold within 24 hours of harvest. For the earth, local-food production means a lot less energy waste and pollution. In the US, most fruits and vegetable travel an average of 1500 miles from the farm to your plate. You can track your zucchini's journey at www.foodroutes.org. Let's look at it another way: Only about 10% of the fossil-fuel energy used in the world's food system goes into production; the other 90% goes into packaging, transportation, and marketing. All this for a salad! So here's how you can become a "locavore":

Know your suppliers. Nearly every community has a farmers' market where you can ask questions and support your local growers. Do they use pesticides, hormones or genetically modified seeds? Ask them in person. You can also become a member of a Community Supported Agriculture (CSA) farm and commit to sharing both the burden of a tough growing season and the benefits of a great crop. Find local growers and CSA farms at www.localharvest.org.

Slow down. The Slow Food Movement is an international response to the damage fast food has done to our health and our palates. Founded in Italy in 1986 to preserve local fresh food and cultural cuisine traditions, Slow Food has chapters in over 100 countries.

Check out www.slowfoodusa.org to see if there's a chapter (or "convivium") near you. If not, start one and invite your friends along to savor the flavor of your local delicacies.

Save the seeds! Buy "heirloom" varieties of food – strains that have been passed down through generations. Many are unique to local areas and are naturally hardy and disease resistant. Best of all, they taste great. These are the flavors that our great grandparents baked into their pies. Unfortunately, many varieties have been lost, but those that remain increase the biodiversity of our gardens. Seed Savers Exchange (www.seedsavers.org) even offers heirloom seeds for sale.

Just say no to the Global Grocery. Let your grocery or your favorite restaurant know that you'd like them to carry local produce, meats and dairy products. They might be doing it already: Chefs are big fans of local food because they know just how good it tastes. If your local businesses are already locavores, they'll appreciate a thumbs-up. If not, let them know that you want to them to make an effort for the earth. They may even appreciate some of your know-how.

Fair prices for fresh food. For every dollar we spend on conventional food, only about 18 cents goes to the grower; the rest goes to middlemen. By contrast, money spent on local food stays in our communities and gives farmers a competitive edge in the marketplace. Heirloom, organic and local foods may cost a bit more, but let's think of it as a good-food premium, one that goes directly towards the preservation of our planet. When local food becomes the norm, prices will come down.

What bounty awaits you just outside your front door?

MONTH

The More the Merrier

❦

Let your neighbors know that you're collecting items to donate to local schools, clubs, scout groups or day care centers and ask them to throw a few things on the pile.

E-ROUNDUP TIME

Feeling a little weighed down by all that electronic clutter? Have an "e-cycling" day at your school or office to collect unwanted electronics. E-cycling Central (www.eiae.org) can help you find a recycling site in your town for disposing of all those computers and dead cell phones.

PRIDE OF PLACE

Let your local representatives know that you'd like to organize a clean-up event and ask if they'll get on board with you. In just a few hours, you can clear walking trails, plant trees and flowers in local parks, or add sustainable plants to existing landscapes – You'll encourage community participation and lots of local pride. You might even find your projects written up in the local paper!

GREEN ORGANIZING

Organize a fundraiser for your favorite green organizations. You'll be surprised how many local merchants and officials will be happy to volunteer their skills or goods to your cause.

A PROPER BURIAL

Most batteries end up
in the landfill, where
they leach dangerous
heavy metals into the
soil and groundwater.
Start a battery collection
box in your school,
office or town. Many
organizations offer
battery-recycling
mailing services for a
small fee (check out
www.batteryrecycling.
com) or you can take the
batteries to a recycling
site on your own (go
to www.earth911.org
for locations).

Volunteering

The more you learn about the environment, the more you'll want to explore new ways you can make a difference. Volunteering can take your green commitment to the next level. From down the street to across the globe, organizations everywhere need volunteers to do, well, just about everything you can imagine: Whether it's cleaning up coast lines, organizing eco-tours or giving talks at schools about the importance of sustainable living, you're needed.

Focus your search by using the Internet. Most organizations have extensive web sites that give a good overview of what they do and what they're looking for. If you're interested in volunteering as a group, gather interested members together and decide the amount of time and resources everyone is able to commit. Organizations such as Amizade (www.amizade.org) and the Student Conservation Association (www.thesca.org) can help fit volunteer opportunities to the particular interests or abilities of you or your group. There really is something out there for everyone.

Think globally, act locally. Lots of local organizations, such as the Kiwanis, Rotary Club, YWCA and YMCA, sponsor community beautification projects that help clear vegetation, plant flowers and trees, and landscape parks and common areas. Keep your eye on the local paper or bulletin board for green activities coming up. Check out the National Recycling Coalition (www.nrc-recycle.org) for recycling events where folks can drop off electronics, paper, ink cartridges and used appliances. If they're coming to your town, why not help get the word out by sending out emails, putting up flyers (on recycled paper, of course!) and telling your neighbors. And if nothing much seems to be happening, think about what you can initiate on your own. Just holding a recycling drive on your block will get a lot of people talking and thinking green.

Get out there. Nationally and internationally, the choices are almost overwhelming: Archaeology, zoology, plant conservation, endangered animals, and ecological data analysis are just a few areas where volunteers are needed. Amizade, for example, is one of many organizations that offer volunteer programs from Washington D.C. to Brazil to Tanzania. They also offer course credit, internships and service-learning for high school and college students. If you want to get your hands dirty while learning more about organic farming, visit World-Wide Opportunities on Organic Farms (www.wwoof.org), who host volunteers at farms in dozens of countries.

Really, there are so many opportunities out there that if you do an Internet search for "Green Volunteer," you'll be knocked right out of your chair.

Be a virtual volunteer. Your computer puts you in touch with just about everyone who's anyone in power. Check your state and local websites and see what your representatives are up to. Don't like it? Write them a letter or give them a call. Do like it? Let them know that you appreciate their earth-positive work. You can find your state and local representatives and learn about their positions at www.vote-smart.org. You can also tell them about any new environmental concerns you may have. This is your right as a constituent – your leaders are waiting to hear from you!

Your computer skills can also help your favorite organizations stay on top of their data collection and other clerical tasks. Just ask them if there's anything you can do to help.

Going green is addictive: You start by making a few changes in your own world, and soon you find that you've got a whole lot more to share with the planet. What gift can you give the earth today?

Green Resources and Websites

Green Science, Research and Policy

Learn about the science behind global warming, carbon emissions and environmental policies. Visit the Union of Concerned Scientists at www.ucsusa.org.

Find out the very latest news about environmental laws and policies, both in the US and internationally. Visit the Natural Resources Defense Counsel at www.nrdc.org.

Investing in Green Energy

Learn about carbon offsets and "green certificates," for individuals and businesses. Visit:

- The Department of Energy's Green Power Network, at www.eere.energy.gov/greenpower,
- Green-e, at www.green-e.org,
- NativeEnergy, at www.nativeenergy.com, or
- www.greentagsusa.org.

Sustainable Energy and Goods Production

See if your electricity is produced from coal from mountain top removal. Go to www.ilovemountains.org.

Learn more about fair trade and sustainable food production. Visit TransFair USA at www.transfairusa.org.

Find out if your meat and dairy products have the "Certified Humane Raised & Handled" label. Go to www.certifiedhumane.com.

Learn how you can purchase sustainably produced forest goods and support responsible forest and land management. Visit the Forest Stewardship Council at www.fscus.org.

Learn about sustainable agriculture and land-use practices. Visit the Rainforest Alliance at www.rainforest-alliance.org.

Food and Product Safety

Find out how safe household, cosmetic and food products are. Visit www.ewg.org.

Learn which products have been approved for their safety and environmental sensitivity. Go to www.greenseal.org.

Find out how safe your seafood is. Visit Monterey Bay Aquarium at www.mbayaq.org.

Learn how much mercury is in your fish. Go to www.gotmercury.org.

Green Gardening

Save your seeds, buy heirloom seed varieties, and learn about encouraging crop diversity. Visit the Seed Savers Exchange at www.seedsavers.org.

Find pesticide alternatives at www.beyondpesticides.org.

Buy No Mow lawn mix at www.prairienursery.com.

Recycling

Learn about what, how and where to recycle. Visit:

- E-cycling Central, at www.eiae.org,
- www.earth911.org,
- www.nrc-recycle.org, or
- www.batteryrecycling.com (offers battery-recycling mailing service for small fee).

Cut down on all those credit card offers. Call 1-888-5OPT OUT.

Green Workplaces

Learn about LEED-certified buildings. Visit the U.S. Green Building Council at www.usgbc.org.

Find out what plants can help keep your workplace clean. Go to www.coopext.colostate.edu/4DMG/Plants/clean.htm.

Green Schools

Learn how teachers can integrate a compost bin into classroom activities. Visit Cornell University at www.css.cornell.edu/compost/schools.html.

Find out how to bring healthy, sustainable eating habits to school cafeterias. Visit Farm to School at www.farmtoschool.org.

For teachers: Get some great green lesson ideas. Visit the Center for Ecoliteracy at www.ecoliteracy.org.

Help kids identify green problems at their schools and become more involved in environmental issues. Go to www.nrdc.org/greensquad.

Transportation

Find out how environmentally friendly your car is. Look at the EPA's Green Vehicle Guide at www.epa.gov/greenvehicles.

Learn about alternative car fuels. Go to www.epa.gov/ebtpages/pollenergycleanfuels.html.

Get information on car sharing. Visit www.zipcar.com.

Local and Organic Food

Learn about local producers and Community Supported Agriculture subscriptions in your community. Visit:

• The Robyn Van En Center, Wilson College, at www.wilson.edu/csasearch, or

• Local Harvest, at www.localharvest.org.

Learn about the state of agriculture and farming in your community and around the country. Visit the American Farmland Trust at www.farmland.org.

Track your food's journey at www.foodroute.org.

Find a Slow Food convivium and learn about the Slow Food movement at www.slowfoodusa.org.

Volunteering

Find green volunteer opportunities around the country and the world. Visit:

- Amizade, at www.amizade.org,
- Student Conservation Association, at www.thesca.org, and
- World-Wide Opportunities on Organic Farms, at www.wwoof.org.

Green and Sustainable Consumer Information

Make informed choices about everyday products. Visit:

- www.thegreenguide.com,
- www.wecanlivegreen.com,
- www.newdream.org, and
- www.earth911.org (just some of the tons of information they have on green issues)

Miscellaneous Resources

Find out more about urban sprawl. Go to www.sierraclub.org/sprawl.

Write or call your state and federal representatives. Go to www.vote-smart.org.

General information on all things green:

- www.treehugger.com.

For environmental news and commentary:

- www.grist.org.

Phipps can be reached on the web at www.phipps.conservatory.org.

About Phipps Conservatory and Botanical Gardens

Phipps Conservatory and Botanical Gardens opened in 1893, a gift to the City of Pittsburgh by wealthy industrialist Henry Phipps, who envisioned a place "that will prove a source of instruction as well as pleasure to the people." Since the privatization of Phipps in 1993, the original vision has flourished through an aggressive multi-phase plan where an appreciation for plant life is balanced with a strong determination to pioneer and showcase the use of sustainable building practices and operations. The original 13-room Victorian glasshouse is anchored with the first LEED-certified visitor center in a public garden, and a new Tropical Forest Conservatory – the most energy efficient conservatory in the world.

By staying true to its original vision, Phipps is now one of the premier horticultural display conservatories and a recognized award winner and leader in green building practices and sustainable operations. Phipps is known as the Green Heart of Pittsburgh and one of the greenest gardens in the world.

Our Mission Statement

To inspire and educate visitors with the beauty and importance of plants, to advance sustainability and worldwide biodiversity through action and research, and to celebrate our historic glasshouse.

Acknowledgments

Thank you to the Board of Trustees of Phipps Conservatory and Botanical Gardens for making sustainability a key component of Phipps' mission statement and for all its support for our green efforts.

A special thanks to the following Phipps staff who contributed their time, talents and expertise to the Green Journal . . .
Richard V. Piacentini, Margie Radebaugh, Erika Ninos, Laura Tobin Thompson, Heather Mikulas, Michael Sexuaer and Jessica Romano.

Thank you to Paul Kelly of St. Lynn's Press for his inspiration and for working with us to make this book a reality.

And thank you to Abby Dees, our editor at St. Lynn's Press, for all her patience, guidance, fine-tuning and wordsmithing.